Record Breakers

A CHAPTER BOOK

BY CATHERINE NICHOLS

children's press®

A Division of Scholastic Inc.
New York Toronto London Auckland Sydney
Mexico City New Delhi Hong Kong
Danbury, Connecticut

For Jay

The author would like to thank all those who gave their time and knowledge to help with this book. In particular, special thanks go to Bob Kersee, Rob Rains, and Peter Kessler.

Library of Congress Cataloging-in-Publication Data

Nichols, Catherine.
  Record breakers : a chapter book / by Catherine Nichols.
    p. cm. – (True tales)
Includes bibliographical references and index.
  ISBN 0-516-23732-2 (lib. bdg.)   0-516-24689-5 (pbk.)
  1. Athletes—United States—Biography—Juvenile literature. I. Title. II. Series.

GV697.A1N47 2004
796'.092'2—dc22

                              2004004935

CONTENTS

INTRODUCTION

A swimmer plunged into icy cold water and set off to swim to the opposite shore. A runner raced down a track and jumped into a pit of sand. A baseball player hit a ball as hard as he could and sent it soaring. A golfer swung his club at a tiny ball and watched as it sank into a hole.

Each of these athletes was attempting to break a long-standing record. Many years ago, Gertrude Ederle became the first woman to swim the English Channel. Jackie Joyner-Kersee set records in track and field that have yet to be broken. Mark McGwire swatted seventy home runs during the 1998 season and became baseball's home run king. Tiger Woods won an important golf **tournament** by an amazing twelve points.

It is not easy to break a record. It takes dedication, courage, and determination. Each athlete in this book has those qualities in abundance.

CHAPTER ONE

QUEEN OF THE SEAS

Gertrude Ederle had been swimming in the cold, choppy water for almost nine hours. Early in the morning of August 18, 1925, she had started her 21-mile (34-kilometer) journey. She still had another 7 miles (11 kilometers) to go. If she made it, she would become the first woman to swim the English Channel successfully.

Suddenly, a huge wave crashed over Gertrude. She swallowed sea water and stopped to spit it out.

Gertrude Ederle

A view of the English Channel from Dorset, England

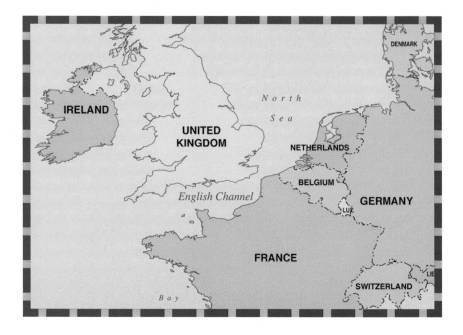

In the boat that was trailing her, her coach, Jabez Wolffe, was concerned. Believing that Gertrude was unable to continue, he pulled her from the water. She fought and cried, but it was too late. According to the rules, Jabez had disqualified Gertrude once he touched her.

Gertrude was not someone to give up her dreams. She was determined to be the first woman to cross the English Channel, a body of water that separates England and France. The English Channel has powerful **currents** that make it difficult to swim.

From the start, Gertrude never let **obstacles** (OB-stih-kuls) stand in her way.

Born in New York City on October 23, 1906, she was the third of six children. Her parents were German immigrants.

When Gertrude was seven years old, she almost drowned. Her father decided she needed to learn how to swim. To teach her, he tied a long rope around her waist. Then, from a pier, he lowered her into the water. Gertrude kicked and paddled while her father held onto the rope.

Soon Gertrude was an **accomplished** swimmer. Four years after learning how to swim, she swam the 800-yard freestyle in 13 minutes 19 seconds. At age twelve, she became the youngest person to break a world record.

Gertrude exercised to stay in shape for swimming.

1924 United States Women's Olympic Swim Team

The following year, Gertrude joined the Women's Swimming Association on New York's Lower East Side. Gertrude won her first long-distance race at age fourteen. She swam from Manhattan Beach to Brighton Beach in a 3.5-mile (5.6-kilometer) race. By age seventeen, she had eighteen world swimming records.

The 1924 Summer Olympic Games were held in Paris, France. Gertrude was there as one of the women swimmers representing the United States. She brought home three medals, one gold and two bronze.

After Gertrude failed in her first attempt to swim the English Channel, she fired Jabez and hired Thomas Burgess. Thomas was the second man to swim the English Channel successfully. Only five people had made it across, all of them men.

On August 6, 1926, a little after seven o'clock in the morning, Gertrude plunged into the icy cold waters from Cape Gris-Nez in France. Her destination, Kingsdown, England, was 21 miles (34 kilometers) away.

Gertrude had prepared carefully for her swim. She wore a two-piece bathing suit that she and her sister had designed. On her head was a bright red bathing cap. Goggles protected her eyes. Melted candle wax had been placed around the outer rims to seal the goggles so that no water could leak through. Before entering the water, Gertrude's body was covered with a combination of lanolin, petroleum, olive oil, and lard. The grease would help keep her body warm and

Gertrude shakes a well-wisher's hand before starting her swim.

protect her from jellyfish stings.

Gertrude wasn't alone in the water. Two small boats followed her to make sure she was safe. In the first boat sat her father, her sister, and her coach. In the second boat were photographers and newspaper reporters. Everyone wanted to know if Gertrude would make it this time.

Not everyone believed that she could. Many people at that time thought that women were too weak to swim such a long distance. One newspaper writer declared that Gertrude's earlier failure to swim the English Channel proved this.

If most newspaper writers didn't believe in Gertrude, her family and friends did. As Gertrude swam, her sister and other people on the boat sang to her. They sang popular tunes of the day, such as "Let Me Call You Sweetheart" and "Yes, We Have No Bananas." The music kept Gertrude's spirits up.

That afternoon the weather turned bad. It began to rain. Strong, gusting winds made it hard to swim. One of Gertrude's legs stiffened and she had trouble kicking with it. Her coach pleaded with her to give up. Gertrude refused.

After more than 14.5 hours of swimming, she reached Kingsdown. She had done it.

While Gertrude swam, her sister and others watched from a boat.

Not only had she become the first woman to swim the English Channel, she had broken the men's record by almost two hours!

Back in New York, a parade was held in Gertrude's honor. Two million people lined up along the sidewalks of lower Manhattan to cheer her.

Unfortunately, Gertrude's hearing might have been damaged from her cold-water swim. Within a few years she was partially deaf. Later, she became completely deaf. Gertrude did not let her loss of hearing stop her. No longer able to swim as a **professional**, she taught swimming to deaf children. She also worked as a dress designer.

No matter what she did, though, Gertrude never forgot her great accomplishment or her love of swimming. The Queen of the Seas, as she was called, once told an interviewer, "I was very happy when I was swimming. I could have gone on and on."

On November 30, 2003, Gertrude Ederle died. She was ninety-eight years old.

A parade for Gertrude snaked down Broadway in New York City.

CHAPTER TWO

FIRST LADY OF TRACK AND FIELD

It was the second day of the women's **heptathlon** (hep-TATH-lon), a demanding contest made up of seven events. Jackie Joyner-Kersee was competing in her first Olympic Games. The first day had gone well and she was in the lead. The next event was the long jump, her best event. A sore **hamstring** kept her from jumping her best. Jackie slipped into second place. The leader was now Glynis Nunn of Australia.

Jackie Joyner-Kersee

Jackie is a fierce competitor.

The last event, the 800-meter dash, would determine the winner. Although her hamstring still bothered her, Jackie gave it her all. As they raced down the track, Glynis sprinted ahead of the pack. Jackie, her arms pumping, tried to catch up. Instead, she came in second, .33 seconds behind Nunn.

The points for all the events in the heptathlon were added together. Jackie had lost the gold medal by five points. Although she had competed with a sore hamstring, Jackie did not use her condition as an excuse. She told others that it wasn't the injury that had cost her the gold medal. It was her "mentality." Jackie said, "I doubted my capabilities."

At the heptathlon ceremony, Jackie stood on the platform and proudly accepted her silver medal. She knew that in four years there would be another Olympic Games. When it came, she would be ready.

Jacqueline Joyner was born on March 3, 1962, in East St. Louis, Illinois. She was named after the nation's first lady, Jacqueline Kennedy, wife of President John Kennedy. Jackie's grandmother claimed that when her granddaughter grew up, she too would be "the first lady of something."

Jacqueline Kennedy

As a child, Jackie had plenty of energy. She threw herself into sports. At a local community center, she ran track and practiced the long jump. When she was just twelve years old, she jumped an amazing 16 feet 9 inches (5 meters 23 centimeters).

Jackie as a member of UCLA's women's basketball team

In high school, Jackie was on the honor roll. She also competed in volleyball, basketball, and track. During her senior year, Jackie tried out for a place on the Olympics long jump team. Unfortunately, she didn't make the team. Later that year, she graduated in the top ten percent of her class. After looking into different colleges, she decided to accept a basketball **scholarship** (SKAH-ler-ship) from UCLA. During her freshman year, Jackie was called back to Illinois with terrible news. Her mother was ill with **meningitis** (meh-nun-JY-tis), a disease of the brain. By the time Jackie flew home, her mother was in a coma. She died without ever waking up.

Jackie was heartbroken, but she knew that her mother would want her to continue her studies. Back at college, she confided in one of the track coaches, Bob Kersee.

Bob thought Jackie had the ability to do very well in the heptathlon. In 1981, Bob Kersee took over as Jackie's sole coach in track and field.

Bob trained Jackie in the seven events of the heptathlon. They are: the 100-meter hurdles, the high jump, the shot put, the 200-meter race, the long jump, the javelin throw, and the 800-meter race. Soon she was setting new college records in the heptathlon.

When she jumps, Jackie looks as if she is flying through the air.

Jackie began training for the 1984 Olympic Games. A year before the Games, she was diagnosed with **asthma** (AZ-muh). Doctors told her that if she gave up sports, her condition would improve. Quitting was never an option for Jackie. Instead, she took medication to help her breathe and avoided training outdoors on smoggy days.

In 1985, while they were at a baseball game, Bob proposed to Jackie. The following year they were married. Even though he was now her husband, Bob continued to coach Jackie.

During the Goodwill Games in Moscow, Jackie broke the world heptathlon record by more than 200 points with a score of 7,148.

Jackie with her husband and coach, Bob Kersee

Jackie competing in the long jump during the 1988 Olympics

Twenty-six days later she broke her own record, racking up 7,161 points. Jackie still wasn't through. At the Olympic trials in Indianapolis, she broke her record yet again. This time she scored 7,215 points.

Jackie arrived at the 1988 Olympics in Seoul, Korea. She was hungry for the gold medal that had gotten away from her in 1984. She won the first event, the 100-meter hurdles, easily. Then, during the high jump, Jackie strained a **tendon** in her knee.

Jackie put ice on her knee to bring down the swelling. The next day, she seemed as fit as ever. Except for the javelin throw, she sailed through the rest of her events. She ended up winning the heptathlon and setting a new world record. For the fourth time in two years, Jackie broke her own record with a score of 7,291!

Jackie took to the medal stand twice, both times to receive gold medals. One gold medal was for winning the heptathlon. The second was for the long jump.

Jackie competed in the next two Olympics, as well. In 1992, she brought home another gold medal in the heptathlon and a bronze in the long jump. In 1996, she injured her hamstring again. She still managed to win a bronze medal in the long jump, however. Two years later, at the age of thirty-six, Jackie retired from professional sports.

Jackie once said that she liked the heptathlon because "it shows you what you're made of." Jackie Joyner-Kersee has not only shown herself what she's made of. She's shown the world!

Jackie celebrates winning the long jump at the 1988 Olympics.

CHAPTER THREE

HOME RUN HERO

On September 8, 1998, Steve Trachsel of the Chicago Cubs pitched to Mark McGwire of the St. Louis Cardinals. Mark responded by hitting a home run. This was no ordinary home run. This was the big one, his sixty-second of the season. As his bat connected with the ball, Mark McGwire broke one of baseball's most unbreakable records.

Mark McGwire

**Mark McGwire rounding first base after
hitting his sixty-second home run**

27

Babe Ruth

Before Mark, Roger Maris held the record for the most home runs in one season. Roger, a New York Yankee, had hit sixty-one home runs way back in 1961. Like Mark, Roger had yanked the record away from a former Yankee and one of the greatest sluggers of all time, Babe Ruth. Babe had hit his sixtieth home run in 1927.

Now the record was Mark's. As he jogged around the bases, Mark was so overcome by what he had accomplished that he missed first base. He had to go back and touch it for the home run to count. Then he headed for home plate, where his cheering teammates awaited him. So did the bat boy, who happened to be Mark's eleven-year-old son, Matthew.

Although Mark is known as a powerful hitter, he started his career as a pitcher.

Mark was eight years old when he first began playing ball. Back then, he wasn't that good a hitter. Perhaps one reason was that he couldn't see the ball clearly. After he was fitted with glasses, Mark's hitting improved. By the time he was ready for Little League, he hit a home run his first time up at bat. As starting pitcher for his team, he carried them to victory for three years straight.

Mark's first love wasn't baseball, though. It was golf. In his second year of high school, he had to make a decision: baseball or golf. Both sports were played in the spring, so he could only play on one team. Mark chose golf.

Although he enjoyed playing golf, Mark discovered he missed pitching. The following year, in 1980, he returned to baseball and stayed. Mark remained a pitcher all through high school. He proved himself to be a top player, and a college in southern California offered him a scholarship. It wasn't until his second year in college that he decided to stop pitching and devote himself to hitting.

After college, Mark was drafted by the Oakland Athletics. He was now a

 professional baseball player. Over the next fourteen years, Mark impressed his teammates and fans with his abilities. Although injuries kept him out of most of the 1993 and 1994 seasons, he battled back from them and came out stronger than ever. Then, in 1997, with only two months to go in the

Mark joined Oakland's major league team in 1986.

season, Mark was traded to the St. Louis Cardinals. Mark finished the 1997 season with some impressive numbers. He had fifty-eight home runs that year, hitting twenty-four of them for the Cardinals in fifty-one games.

The 1998 baseball season got off to a great start for Mark McGwire. On his team's opening day, he hit a grand slam. A little more than a week later, he hit three homers in one game. By the end of April, he had slammed eleven home runs. By the end of May, he had twenty-seven.

Throughout their race to win the home run record, Mark and Sammy supported one another.

As June approached, baseball fans began whispering about a new home run record. Would Mark be the one to break Roger Maris's record? Sports reporters compared Mark's home-run pace to Roger's and Babe's. As the season went on, Mark continued to hit. Now, though, he had a **rival**, Sammy Sosa of the Chicago Cubs.

Unlike Mark, Sammy had been having an average season. He hit six home runs in April and seven in May. He exploded in June, hitting twenty home runs. It was a record. In July, he hit nine more, including two **grand slams**. For a few minutes on August 19, Sammy actually took the lead in the race for the most home runs. He hit number forty-eight in a game against the Cardinals. Mark did not let Sammy remain in the lead for long. In the same game, he hit numbers forty-eight and forty-nine.

By September, the last month in the regular season, Mark and Sammy were tied. They each had fifty-five home runs. After Mark broke the home run record with sixty-two home runs, the excitement continued to grow. The season was not over yet. How many more home runs would Mark hit? What about Sammy? With fifty-eight home runs, Sammy was still in the race.

As the scoreboard shows, on September 8, 1998, Mark had sixty-two home runs. Sammy had fifty-eight. **33**

Just five days later, Sammy tied Mark's record of sixty-two home runs. For the rest of September, the two sluggers battled for the right to hold the record of most home runs in a season. As soon as Mark set a new record, Sammy would match him. On September 25, Sammy held the title of home run king for 45 minutes. Then Mark tied Sammy by swatting number sixty-six in a game against the Montreal Expos.

The two players went into the final weekend of the season tied with sixty-six home runs. That's when Mark left Sammy behind for good. On Saturday, he hit two home runs. The following day, he hit two more. Mark McGwire finished the 1998 baseball season with seventy home runs!

Records, however, are made to be broken. Mark's record was no different. In 2001, Barry Bonds of the San Francisco Giants hit seventy-three home runs in one season. For now, Barry's record stands.

**Mark celebrates after hitting his
sixty-second home run of the season.**

CHAPTER FOUR

TIGER MANIA

It was the final **round** of the 1997 **Masters Championship** in Augusta, Georgia. Tiger Woods had been through three days of demanding play. Round one's first nine holes had been especially embarrassing. He had made four **bogeys** (BOW-geez). Tiger refused to give up. He rebounded and began making his shots. By the end of the first round, he was three shots **shy** of the lead. The following day, his excellent play continued. He took the lead and kept it.

Now Tiger Woods stood on the eighteenth **green**, ready to make his last shot. He swung his **putter,** and rolled the ball into the cup.

Tiger Woods

With that last shot, Tiger Woods made history, winning the **prestigious** tournament with the lowest score and by the widest margin ever. At age twenty-one, he also became the youngest Masters winner. Perhaps most importantly, he became the first African American to do so.

After winning, Tiger walked over to his father, Earl Woods, and hugged him. Both men began to cry. Without his father's support and encouragement, Tiger would very likely not be at the Masters. Earl had encouraged his son's love of the game from the time Tiger was a baby. When Tiger was six months old, he would sit in his high chair in the family's garage and watch Earl practice hitting golf balls.

Tiger holds his Masters trophy.

When Tiger was a toddler, his father sawed down one of his old putters and let Tiger hit

Tiger has a close relationship with his mother and father.

the ball. He was surprised at how good Tiger was. While still in training pants, Tiger would call his father at work and beg him to take him to the golf course.

Before long, people began to hear about Tiger Woods. When he was only two years old, Tiger appeared on a television talk show. He putted against Bob Hope, a famous comedian and **amateur** (A-muh-tur) golfer, and won! At age five, he was written up in a golf magazine and appeared on another television show, *That's Incredible!* Tiger Mania had begun.

For his parents, Tiger Mania began on December 30, 1975, the day of his birth.

Tiger had an impressive swing from an early age.

He was named Eldrick Thon Woods. His father called him Tiger in honor of a friend with the same nickname. The friend had saved Earl's life when Earl was a soldier during the Vietnam War. Earl had always admired his friend's bravery.

Tiger lived up to his namesake. The child of an African-American father and Asian mother, Tiger grew up in an all-white neighborhood. Although he was sometimes teased by his classmates, he refused to let other people's taunts bother him.

As Tiger grew, Earl played a big part in shaping his son's golf game. Besides giving him helpful pointers, Earl taught his son mental toughness. This meant doing things like making sudden noises as Tiger got ready to swing. Sometimes he'd stand in front of Tiger and tell him he was a tree. He knew that when Tiger was a professional golfer, there would be many distractions. Tiger had to be ready to focus on his game and not let the distractions get to him.

Earl's approach must have worked. By age fifteen, Tiger was the youngest United

As a teenager, Tiger enjoyed spending
time with his father on the golf course.

States junior amateur **champion** (CHAM-pee-un) in golf history. At age eighteen, he accepted a golf scholarship from Stanford University in California. His first year there, Tiger won an important college tournament. That year he also won the United States Amateur Championship. He went on to win it three years in a row, becoming the first player in the history of golf to do so.

In 1996, when Tiger was twenty years old, he turned pro. Just one short year later, he had won the Masters. At the end of that tournament, after he had embraced his father, Tiger stopped to hug one more person. He was Lee Elder, an important figure in the history of golf. Lee was the first African American invited to play the Masters. Lee had paved the way for minorities.

Today, Tiger remains a major force in golf. As golfer Tommy Tolles once said, "The rest of us will just be teeing up for silver medals for the next twenty years." Is Tiger that good? Only time will tell. Meanwhile, his record at the Masters still stands. Any takers?

Tiger hugs his trophy after winning the 100th U.S. Open Golf Championship.

GLOSSARY

accomplished skillful

amateur (A-muh-tur) someone who does something as a hobby, for free

asthma (AZ-muh) a condition that causes difficulty breathing

bogey (BOW-gee) a score of one stroke over average on a golf course

champion (CHAM-pee-un) the best at something

current the movement of water in a river or ocean

grand slam a home run with the bases loaded

green the area of grass surrounding a hole on a golf course

hamstring any of the muscles at the back of the leg

heptathlon (hep-TATH-lon) a contest in which each athlete competes in seven track and field events

Masters Championship an important golf tournament played each year in Georgia

meningitis (meh-nun-JY-tis) an illness in which the areas surrounding the brain become swollen, red, and painful

obstacle (OB-stih-kul) something that is in the way

prestigious very important

professional someone who is paid for what they do

putter a golf club used to hit a ball a short distance

rival someone who tries to beat someone else at something

round eighteen holes of golf

scholarship (SKAH-ler-ship) money given to someone to pay for school

shy short or lacking in something

tendon a band of tissue connecting muscle to bone

tournament a contest played for a championship

FIND OUT MORE

Queen of the Seas
www.msu.edu/~grawbur1/iahweb.html
Learn more about Gertrude Ederle and her historic swim across the English Channel.

First Lady of Track and Field
www.sacbee.com/static/archive/news/projects/people_of_ce
ntury/sports/kersee.html
Read a short biography about Jackie Joyner-Kersee, one of the great women athletes of the century.

Home Run Hero
http://sportsillustrated.cnn.com/baseball/mlb/1998/62/hit6
2/video/movie_1_240.html
Watch a video that shows Mark McGwire hitting the home run that broke Roger Maris's record of the most home runs in a season.

Tiger Mania
www.rolemodel.net/tiger/tiger.htm
Find out why Tiger Woods is a great role model for young people.

More Books to Read

America's Champion Swimmer: Gertrude Ederle by David A. Adler, Gulliver Books/Harcourt, 2000

Home Run Heroes: Big Mac, Sammy & Junior by James Buckley, Jr., DK Publishing, 2001

Jackie Joyner-Kersee: Superwoman by Margaret J. Goldstein and Jennifer Larson, Lerner Publications, 1994

Tiger Woods: Drive to Greatness by Mark Stewart, Millbrook Press, 2001

INDEX

PHOTO CREDITS

MEET THE AUTHOR

Catherine Nichols lives in Jersey City, New Jersey. She has worked in children's publishing as an editor, project manager, and author. She has written many children's books, including sports biographies on Babe Ruth and Jackie Robinson.

While Catherine hasn't broken any records as yet, she does enjoy swimming, biking, and taking her dog, Pablo, for long walks.